Classic Plastic

DOLLS 1945-1965

Cynthia Gaskill

Gold Horse Publishing

Inquiries should be addressed to:
Theriault's Gold Horse Publishing
PO Box 151, Annapolis, Maryland 21404

Art Direction and Design: David W. Hirner
Photography: Robert Bartlett

Props courtesy of:
Nouveau Contemporary Goods, Baltimore, MD
Broadway Antique Market, Baltimore, MD

$39
ISBN: 0-912823-62-3
Printed in Hong Kong

Introduction

What sparks a wave of nostalgia from your childhood? Is it a song on the radio... seeing an old friend...visiting a long-forgotten area or secret hide-away...going through old photographs...or is it the memory of playing with a certain doll?

Today adults in record numbers all over the world are reliving the happiest of times from the past by, once again, obtaining their favorite childhood dolls and toys. Some are again played with and become part of the ever-growing toy chest, others are coveted and placed on display only to be looked at - but don't touch! For some, one could never put a price on such memories, while others view the current popularity as a savvy business opportunity. Whatever your collector style may be, the dolls from our past are a highly emotional collectible, evoking personal remembrances individual to us all.

The criteria for what makes a doll valuable is oddly different to us all. Though the current market dictates that the doll's condition must be perfect and pristine in order to command the highest value, we have witnessed in past months the rise in "sentimental" value and rarity in some dolls, catapulting them into the realms of legendary prices. What becomes a legend most? Obviously, the emotional value attached to it over and above whatever the current market status may be.

The classic examples of modern dolls in this book detail a small amount of today's market variety. There is no doubt, a doll similar to one you played with in an earlier time, somewhere in this volume. Whatever your interest in this ever-changing category of dolls, we wish you many years of happy memories and happy collecting these "Classic Plastic" treasures.

1. American Character Toodles

24". Hard plastic five-piece child body, vinyl head, rooted sandy blonde wig, blue sleep eyes, curled lashes, open pink mouth with teeth. Pink gingham, chintz sundress with matching bonnet, organdy apron, pink nylon panty, satin shoes. Circa 1960. Comes with eight additional pieces of clothing, original box marked #2503 and "The Fun and Play Book" from American Doll & Toy Corp. formerly American Character.

2. American Character Tiny Tears

11". Vinyl five-piece baby body with hard plastic head, rooted tosca hair, blue sleep eyes, brush lashes, open pink mouth with bottle hole. White patterned sunsuit with pink trim and pink/white knit booties. Comes in presentation box with pink/white cotton dress and panty, diaper, bubble pipe, bottle, sponges, tissues and wash cloth. Circa 1960, original box.

3. Little Betsy Wetsy Outfit

Polished cotton print romper and matching bonnet with booties in original box with wardrobe booklet, #9610. Ideal, circa 1957.

4. Madame Alexander Marybel

15". Hard plastic six-piece child body, vinyl head with rooted blonde hair, brown sleep eyes, brush lashes, pink rosebud mouth. Tagged pink satin romper with blue ribbon and lace accents, pink slippers with pom-poms. Original carrying case with medical supplies, plastic casts, crutches, bandages, pox spots and sunglasses. Circa 1958, marked Alexander 1958 on head. Excellent coloring.

5. Arranbee Littlest Angel Walker

11". Hard plastic seven-piece toddler body with head that turns when walked, brunette saran wig with flocked daisy accents, blue sleep eyes, molded lashes, red rosebud mouth. Red and white cotton polka-dot sunsuit with ruffled back panty, nylon panty underneath, white socks and shoes. Circa 1958, head and body both marked R&B. Rich facial coloring.

6. Vogue Littlest Angel Walker

11". Hard plastic seven-piece toddler body with vinyl head that turns when walked, rooted white nylon hair, blue sleep eyes, brush lashes, pink rosebud mouth. Wears nylon panty and white shoes and socks. Circa 1962, #31030 and $3.00 price on box.

5

7. Effanbee Junior Girl Scout
8″. Five-piece vinyl child body, rooted brunette saran hair, brown sleep eyes, molded lashes, orange smiling mouth. Green cotton girl scout uniform with yellow satin tie, nylon panty, green socks, brown shoes and green beanie. Circa 1965, marked Effanbee on head and #11-966 Official Junior Girl Scout Doll on box with $4.50 price tag.

8. American Character Baby Toodles
21″. Nine-piece vinyl baby body, molded hair, blue sleep eyes, brush lashes, pink rosebud mouth with bottle hole. Pink and white cotton romper with button, lace and stitching accents, ornate bonnet, flannel diaper and sandals. Circa 1958. Original box marked Style #22100. Hard-to-find baby in this size and condition.

9. Ideal Thumbelina
19″. Cloth body with vinyl limbs and head, knob at back, rooted tosca saran hair, painted blue eyes, pink open mouth. Tagged blue romper with striped shirt. Circa 1961, original box. When knob is wound she wriggles around and has a crier, realistic modeling of the hands and feet.

10. Horsman Poor Pitiful Pearl

11". Hard plastic and vinyl five-piece child body, rooted tosca hair, grey sleep eyes, pink watermelon smile. Blue cotton print "rags" dress with patch, head scarf, black hose and shoes. Circa 1963. Original box with pretty pink party dress, white socks, shoes and story booklet by award winning cartoonist William Steig.

11. Madame Alexander Chatterbox

24". Five-piece hard plastic and vinyl child body, rooted platinum blonde nylon hair with pink bows, blue sleep eyes, brush lashes, pink rosebud mouth with bottle hole. Tagged pink floral print romper with satin bows, white socks and shoes and instruction sheets. Circa 1961, original box, style #7950. Doll says a variety of phrases via a battery-operated mechanism.

12. Mary-Lu Walker

17". Five-piece hard plastic child walker body, blonde braided wig, green sleep eyes, brush lashes, red open mouth with teeth. One-piece dress with cream top, blue cotton skirt, white socks and shoes, original box. Circa 1955.

13. Vogue Kindergarten Ginny
8". Five-piece hard plastic body, blonde caracul "poodle" wig with blue bow, blue sleep eyes, painted lashes, red mouth. Tagged yellow swiss dot dress with matching panty, eyelet accents, blue socks and snap shoes. Circa 1952, Kindergarten Series #22 Donna with original wrist tag.

14. Vogue Kindergarten Ginny
8". Five-piece hard plastic body, blonde wig with pink bow, blue sleep eyes, painted lashes, red mouth. Tagged pink organdy dress with matching panty, lace trim, pink socks, white shoes. Circa 1952, Kindergarten Series #24, April.

15. Vogue Kindergarten Ginny
8". Five-piece hard plastic body, light brown caracul "poodle" wig, brown sleep eyes, painted lashes, red mouth. Tagged pink polished cotton dress with matching panty, pastel trim, pink socks and shoes, pink straw hat, blue purse. Circa 1952, Kindergarten Series #25 Connie.

16. Vogue Ginny with Box
8". Seven-piece hard plastic walker body, blonde braided saran wig, blue sleep eyes, molded lashes, red mouth. Wears nylon panty, white socks and shoes. Circa 1958, #1003 Ginny in original box.

17. Vogue Ginny with Box
8". Five-piece hard plastic walker body, brown saran hair, blue sleep eyes, molded lashes, red mouth. Blue nylon panty, socks and shoes. Circa 1957, #6102 Ginny walker with original circular wrist tag and box.

18. Vogue Ginny Cowboy

8″. Five-piece hard plastic body, brown mohair wig, brown sleep eyes, painted lashes, pale mouth. Outfit is blue/red plaid flannel shirt attached to black felt pants with curly "chap" front, vinyl vest and cuffs, belt, metal gun, yellow ribbon bandanna, tan felt hat, red snap shoes. Circa 1951, original metal stand included.

19. Vogue Ginny Cowgirl

8″. Five-piece hard plastic body, blonde mohair wig, blue sleep eyes, painted lashes, pale mouth. Outfit is a plaid flannel shirt attached to a vinyl skirt with multi-colored fringe, matching vest and cuffs, yellow bandanna, red knit panty, tan felt hat, green snap shoes. Circa 1951, original wrist tag.

20. Vogue Tiny Miss Ginny

8″. Five-piece hard plastic walker body, brown wig, brown sleep eyes, painted lashes, red mouth. Tagged green floral print cotton dress with matching panty, green felt vest front with flowers and ties, green straw hat. Circa 1954. #42 Tiny Miss Series.

21. Pair of Ginny Suitcases

4 1/4″ x 2″. Pair of cardboard suitcases for Ginny with printed travel destinations. Includes pink cotton nightie and towel, blue floral nightie, blue pom-pom slippers and blue plastic mirror and comb. Circa 1955.

22. Vogue Ginny Walker

8″. Hard plastic five-piece walker body, blonde wig, blue sleep eyes, molded lashes, red mouth. Tagged dress of white top and plaid skirt, red felt jacket and hat with feather, red shoes. Circa 1957, #15C, School Time outfit.

23. Nancy Ann Style Show Doll
18″. Five-piece hard plastic body, blonde curled saran wig, grey sleep eyes, brush lashes, red mouth. Pink taffeta gown with overlay of imported French lace and matching lace bolero jacket (buttons inserted into bustline of gown), attached nosegay, cotton hooped petticoat, stockings and cream satin slippers. Unmarked. Circa 1950, #2404 Sophistication outfit.

24. Nancy Ann Style Show Doll
18″. Five-piece hard plastic body, brown curled saran wig with floral bow, grey sleep eyes, brush lashes, red mouth. Pink satin bodice with beaded accent (buttons inserted into bustline), full double overlay skirt of net and lace with matching cap sleeves, cotton hooped petticoat, stockings and cream satin slippers. Unmarked. Circa 1950, #2903 Opera Night gown with original wrist tag and box.

Nancy Ann Storybook Dolls
From left to right, top to bottom

25. Little Bo Peep #9117
5 1/2″. Five-piece hard plastic body, blonde wig, blue sleep eyes. Turquoise and printed cotton dress, felt hat with flowers, pantaloons, painted black slippers. Circa 1953. Original wrist tag and box.

26. January Girl #162
5 1/2″. Five-piece hard plastic body, carrot-colored wig, blue sleep eyes. Blue nylon and net gown with silver-laced sleeves and floral accent, pink felt hat with ribbon, white panty, painted black slippers. Circa 1953. Original wrist tag and box.

27. Fairy Godmother #132
5 1/2″. Five-piece hard plastic body, carrot-colored wig, blue sleep eyes. White and gold net gown with shawl, paper crown, gold-painted toothpick wand, pantaloons and black painted slippers. Circa 1953. Original wrist tag and box.

28. Silks and Satins #116
5 1/2″. Five-piece hard plastic body, carrot-colored wig, blue sleep eyes. Floral-printed dress and matching pantaloons with red net lace accents, yellow nylon slip, green felt bonnet, black painted slippers. Circa 1953. Original box.

29. January #162
5 1/2″. Five-piece hard plastic body, blonde wig, blue sleep eyes. Gown is as described in #26. Original box with shadow frame front.

30. Lucy Locket #146
5 1/2″. Five-piece hard plastic body, carrot-colored wig, blue sleep eyes. Gown of pink nylon with gold lace accents and flower accent, pantaloons, hair ribbon and heart necklace, painted black slippers. Circa 1953. Original wrist tag and box.

31. Bridesmaid #151
5 1/2″. Five-piece hard plastic body, carrot-colored hair, blue sleep eyes. Gown of purple nylon and tulle with flowers and ribbon accents, silver lace sleeves, net halo bonnet, painted black slippers. Circa 1953. Original wrist tag and box with shadow frame front.

11

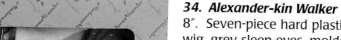

32. Wendy Ann with Box
7 1/2″. Five-piece hard plastic body, tosca wig, grey sleep eyes, molded lashes, red mouth. Tagged white organdy dress with matching slip and panty, red polka-dot pinafore that ties in back, red side-snap shoes, straw bonnet. Circa 1954, with original wrist tag and box.

33. Alexander-kin Walker
8″. Five-piece hard plastic walker body, blonde wig, grey sleep eyes, molded lashes, red mouth. Tagged white organdy dress with red ric-rac trim, white slip and panty, red side-snap shoes, straw bonnet. Circa 1955, #447 Tea Party at Grandma's outfit.

34. Alexander-kin Walker
8″. Seven-piece hard plastic walker body, tosca wig, grey sleep eyes, molded lashes, red mouth. Tagged red and white striped organdy sun dress with matching panty, button accents, lace-edged sun bonnet, red glasses and purse, black shoes. Circa 1957, #338 Dressed for a Hot Morning outfit, in box marked #300.

35. Madame Alexander Kelly Dress
Tagged blue cotton dress with crochet lace trim, button front and satin ribbon in box.

36. Madame Alexander-kin Outfit
Tagged pink cotton nightgown with lace edging, ribbon flower, pair of pink slippers with pom-poms. In box marked #032.

37. Wendy Kin Outfit
Tagged red cotton pleated dress with matching panty, white knit jacket, red straw hat and red purse. In box with FAO Schwarz sticker, circa 1964.

38. Madame Alexander Story Princess
18". Nine-piece hard plastic and vinyl body, brunette curled wig, green sleep eyes, brush lashes, red mouth. Tagged pink nylon gown with tulle overlay and floral accents, white nylon pantalets, stockings, silver slippers, golden braid crown and magic wand. Circa 1956, #1892 The Story Princess Doll from the NBC television shows of the era.

39. Nancy Ann Muffie
7 1/2". Five-piece hard plastic walker body, blonde curled wig, light brown sleep eyes, molded/painted lashes. Pink floral cotton dress with lace accents, white panty and full slip, pink socks and shoes, pink straw hat with flowers, purse. Marked Storybook Dolls California Muffie on back. Circa 1955.

40. Nancy Ann Muffie
7 1/2". Five-piece hard plastic walker body, brunette braided wig, blue sleep eyes, molded/painted lashes, no eyebrows. Blue cotton dress with colored ribbon, nylon panty, Muffie purse. Marked Storybook Dolls California on back. Circa 1953.

41. Nancy Ann Muffie
7 1/2". Five-piece hard plastic walker body, tosca curled wig, brown sleep eyes, molded/painted lashes. Pink nylon panty, white shoes, Muffie purse. Marked Storybook Dolls California Muffie on back. Circa 1955. Original box marked #500C.

42. Nancy Ann Muffie
7 1/2". Seven-piece hard plastic walker body, blonde curled wig, blue sleep eyes, molded/painted lashes. Yellow cotton print dress with lace bib front, cotton panty, green straw hat with flowers, green purse and gloves. Marked Storybook Doll California Muffie on back. Circa 1956.

43. Nancy Ann Storybook Davy Crockett Muffie
7 1/2". Five-piece hard plastic walker body, brown short wig, blue sleep eyes, molded/painted lashes. Brown suedene shirt and pants with cut fringe, belt, fur cap and button. Marked Storybook Doll California Muffie on back. Circa 1955. Hard-to-find outfit.

44. Vogue "Rich Uncle" Trunk for Ginny

12" W. x 9" L. x 4" H. Red paper-covered trunk with quilted lining includes painted-lash Ginny with auburn hair and blue sleep eyes, and six assorted outfits with assorted socks, purses and hair curlers. Circa 1951, catalogue #828. A wonderful presentation piece.

45. Vogue Painted-Eye Ginny

8". Five-piece hard plastic body, brown curled wig, painted blue eyes. Tagged dress of black velvet bodice, pink satin skirt with black flocked design, pink tie shoes, black straw hat. Marked Vogue Doll on back. Circa 1950.

46. Vogue Mistress Mary Ginny

8". Five-piece hard plastic body, blonde curled wig, blue sleep eyes, painted lashes. Tagged blue taffeta pinafore with attached pantaloons, flowers at hem, lace accents, pink straw bonnet with matching flowers, pink front-snap shoes, pink watering can. Circa 1952 Mistress Mary from the Frolicking Fables Series. Exquisite condition for this desirable model.

47. Vogue Prince Charming Ginny

7 1/2". Five-piece hard plastic body, short blonde wig, painted blue eyes. Tagged cotton shirt with ruffled front, attached blue knit leggings, blue satin vest, matching cap with large feather, blue slippers. Holds a blue satin pillow with gold shoe on it. Circa 1950 Prince Charming from the Cinderella Group with original metal Vogue stand.

48. Ideal Shirley Temple with Box
19″. Five-piece hard vinyl body, light brown curled, rooted wig, soft vinyl face with hazel flirty and sleep eyes, brush lashes. Tagged yellow nylon dress with black trim and attached slip, floral accent at waist, original name pin, cotton panty, black side-snap shoes, pearl necklace. Circa 1957, #1420 in larger size. Includes original gold star box, wrist tags and booklet, also includes miniature travel case with Shirley signature logo.

49. Ideal Shirley Temple
17″. Five-piece hard vinyl body, light brown curled, rooted wig, hazel sleep eyes, brush lashes. Pink nylon dress with embroidered trim, matching panty, signature pin, black shoes, straw bonnet. Circa 1957 with original wrist tag and white flat purse.

50. Ideal Shirley Temple with Box

12". Five-piece hard vinyl body, light brown curled, rooted wig, hazel sleep eyes, molded lashes. Dress is pink nylon bodice with lace accents, long pleated skirt of white nylon with attached pink cotton skirt and matching panty, floral corsage, golden slippers. Circa 1958 in original picture box with wrist tag.

51. Ideal Shirley Temple with Box

12". Five-piece hard vinyl body, light brown curled, rooted wig with pink bow, hazel sleep eyes, molded lashes. Tagged pink nylon slip with matching panty, front-snap black shoes. Circa 1957 in original gold star box.

52. Ideal Shirley Temple

15". Five-piece hard vinyl body, light brown curled, rooted wig with pink bow, hazel sleep eyes, brush lashes. Tagged pink nylon dress with floral print, lace accents, attached pink slip, panty, white shoes. Circa 1957 with original signature pin and black purse.

53. Effanbee Honey Majorette

17". Five-piece hard plastic body, auburn mohair wig, blue sleep eyes, brush lashes. Red and white nylon majorette uniform with matching cape, flannel hat, gold wooden baton, gold foil boots. Marked Effanbee on back of head. Circa 1952. #7624 Majorette outfit in original blue box with silver striped lid.

17

54. Alexander Little Genius with Box

7 1/2". Five-piece vinyl baby body, hard plastic head, blonde wig, grey sleep eyes, molded lashes, rosebud mouth with opening. Tagged dress with blue rosebud print, matching cap, eyelet slip, panty, knit booties with flower garter. Circa 1956-1961. With bottle, wrist tag and box.

55. Alexander Little Genius

7 1/2". Five-piece vinyl baby body, hard plastic head, blonde wig, grey sleep eyes, molded lashes, rosebud mouth with opening. Two-piece pink striped play outfit, knit booties, flower garter. Circa 1961, #105 Play Pen Suit with original bottle.

56. Alexander Little Genius
7 1/2″. Five-piece vinyl baby body, hard plastic head, blonde wig, grey sleep eyes, molded lashes, rosebud mouth with opening. Tagged pink striped shift with lace and flower accents, eyelet cap and matching panty, knit booties with flower garter. Circa 1961 with box.

57. Alexander Littlest Kitten with Box
7″. Five-piece vinyl baby body, vinyl head, platinum rooted hair with pink bow, grey sleep eyes, molded lashes. Tagged pink cotton romper with lace accents, knit booties, pink ribbon ties. Marked Alex Doll Co on head. Circa 1963. Outfit #525 with bottle and original box.

58. Alexander Littlest Kitten with Box
7″. Five-piece vinyl baby body, vinyl head, rooted blonde hair, grey sleep eyes, molded lashes. Tagged pink cotton dress with ribbed organdy bodice and floral accent, flannel diaper, knit booties. Marked Alex Doll Co on head. Circa 1964. Outfit #832 with extra white organdy dress and cap, original box.

59. Madame Alexander "Little Women"
11″. Five-piece hard plastic bodies, Lissy face, various hair color, grey sleep eyes, molded lashes. All have tagged outfits consisting of dresses and pinafores over petticoats and pantalets, black side-snap shoes. Circa 1965. All have original wrist booklets.

63. *Effanbee Honey Cinderella with Box*
14″. Five-piece hard plastic body, blonde mohair wig, grey sleep eyes, brush lashes. Pink nylon gown with tulle and gold trim overlay, floral accents and ruffles, matching panty, clear "glass" slippers, gold paper crown. Marked Effanbee on head and back. Circa 1952. Stock #8423 with original box. Hard-to-find smaller-sized doll in wonderfully preserved condition.

64. *Effanbee Honey Prince Charming*
14″. Hard plastic five-piece body, blonde mohair wig, grey sleep eyes, brush lashes. Pink nylon suit of capelet and breeches with gold trim, matching cape and feathered cap, hose. Marked Effanbee on head and body. Circa 1952. Stock #8524, carries original clear "glass" slipper. Excellent, original condition, hard-to-find smaller-sized doll.

65. Effanbee Honey Formal
16 1/2". Hard plastic five-piece body, blonde mohair wig with floral accents, blue sleep eyes, brush lashes. Blue nylon gown with attached full slip, matching panty, black and gold ribbon trim, cream center-snap shoes. Marked Effanbee on head and Effanbee Made in USA on body. Circa 1952.

66. Arranbee Nancy Lee Formal
14". Hard plastic five-piece body, blonde floss wig tied up with velvet ribbons, green sleep eyes, brush lashes. Plaid taffeta gown with diagonally-cut bodice velvet ribbon tie, lace gauntlets, cotton hooped slip and matching panty, gold center-snap shoes. Circa 1952.

67. Arranbee Nancy Lee Formal
14". Hard plastic five-piece body, light brown floss wig tied up with satin ribbon, blue sleep eyes, brush lashes. Floral nylon gown with shoulder ties and ruffle accent, lace gauntlets, floral faux parasol, cotton hooped petticoat and matching panty, gold center-snap shoes. Marked R&B on head. Circa 1952.

68. Vogue Debutante Ginny
7 1/2". Five-piece hard plastic body, blonde curled wig, blue sleep eyes, painted lashes. Tagged pink taffeta dress with organdy laced overlay and floral garland accents (original $4.95 price tag attached), pink panty, straw bonnet with flowers and feathers, pink center-snap shoes. Marked Vogue Doll on back. Circa 1952. #60 Debutante Series "Pamela" in pink box labelled #25 Connie.

69. Vogue Tiny Miss Ginny
8". Five-piece hard plastic body, auburn braided wig, blue sleep eyes, painted lashes. Tagged yellow floral organdy dress with black ribbon trim, lace accents, matching panty, straw bonnet with flower, black center-snap shoes. Marked Vogue Doll on back. Circa 1953. #40 Tiny Miss Series "Wanda".

70. Vogue Tiny Miss Ginny
8". Five-piece hard plastic body, auburn curled wig, blue sleep eyes, painted lashes. Tagged blue organdy dress with floral print, layered waist, lace edging, matching panty, straw hat with flowers, blue center-snap shoes. Marked Vogue Doll on back. Circa 1952. #42 Tiny Miss Series with wrist tag.

71. Vogue Tiny Miss Ginny
8". Five-piece hard plastic body, blonde braided wig, blue sleep eyes, painted lashes. Tagged green and white print dress with matching panty, organdy pinafore with lace edges attached, straw hat with bow, green center-snap shoes. Marked Vogue Doll on back. Circa 1953. #39 Lucy from the Tiny Miss Series.

72. *Vogue Kindergarten Ginny*

8". Five-piece hard plastic body, blonde curled wig with red bow, blue sleep eyes, painted lashes. Tagged red organdy dress with matching panty, lace accents and flower, red center-snap shoes. Marked Vogue Doll on back. Circa 1953. #23 Kay from the Kindergarten Afternoon Series.

73. *Ginny's Pup*

3 1/2" L. x 3 1/2" H. Mohair terrier with brown glass eyes, stitched mouth and nose, neck ribbon, plaid vinyl blanket, original Steiff ear button, black leash. Circa 1954. Catalogue #831, Ginny's pup.

74. *Ginny's fitted Wardrobe Chest*

Presentation set includes a Ginny with auburn curled wig, blue sleep eyes and painted lashes. Includes a green velvet coat and hat, fur muff, floral print dress, hat, cosmetic cape, shoes and various accessories and jewelry. Circa 1954. Catalogue #822, cleverly folds into a larger version of the Ginny suitcase.

23

75. Ideal Toni Walker with Box

14". Five-piece hard plastic walker body, blonde nylon wig with red ribbon, green sleep eyes, brush lashes, fresh facial coloring. Tagged blue cotton dress with attached red polka dot organdy overlay, attached slip and matching panty, white vinyl shoes. Marked Ideal Doll P-90 on head and 90W on back. Circa 1955. Original play wave set, wrist tag and unusual red, white and blue box with Toni label.

76. Ideal Toni Walker with Box

14". Five-piece hard plastic walker body, blonde nylon wig with green ribbon, green sleep eyes, brush lashes, good facial coloring. Green cotton dress with yellow polka-dotted organdy overlay, green trim, white vinyl shoes. Marked P-90 on head and 90W on back. Circa 1955. Original play wave set, wrist tag and box marked #1141.

77. Ideal Toni Bride

14". Five-piece hard plastic body, blonde nylon wig, grey sleep eyes, brush lashes. White nylon gown with lace accents and panniers, attached full cotton petticoat and matching panty, bouquet with ribbon, full-length veil, white center-snap shoes. Circa 1954.

78. Arranbee Nancy Lee Skater
20". Five-piece hard plastic body, blonde mohair wig, blue sleep eyes, brush lashes. Red flannel skating outfit with matching red and tan jacket, fur accent, woven nylon scarf, tan beret, white skates, marked R&B on head. Circa 1952. Original box with label #4106 with excellent coloring in rarer large size.

79. Mary Hoyer Formal with Box
14". Five-piece hard plastic body, brown curled mohair wig, grey sleep eyes, brush lashes. White polished cotton formal with lace accents and floral hem trim, attached organdy underskirt, pearl necklace, straw bonnet, white center-snap shoes, marked original Mary Hoyer Doll in circle on back. Circa 1946-50. Vivid and fresh coloring, original box.

80. Mary Hoyer Formal with Box
14". Five-piece hard plastic body, blonde curled mohair wig, blue sleep eyes, smoky eyeshadow, brush lashes. Tagged aqua taffeta, sleeveless cocktail dress with matching wrap, silver net overlay, nylon panty, hose, beaded necklace, satin center-snap shoes. Marked Mary Hoyer Doll in circle on back. Circa 1946-50. Excellent coloring, original box.

81. Mary Hoyer with Box
14". Five-piece hard plastic body, blonde curled mohair wig, grey sleep eyes, smoky shadow, brush lashes. Tagged pink cotton sundress with green ric-rac trim accenting, matching bonnet, nylon panty, white center-snap shoes. Marked Original Mary Hoyer Doll in circle on back. Circa 1946-50. Vivid coloring, original box.

82. Mary Hoyer with Box
14". Five-piece hard plastic body, blonde curled mohair wig, grey sleep eyes, smoky shadow, brush lashes. Tagged blue cotton playsuit with white piping and removable skirt, white center-snap shoes. Marked Original Mary Hoyer Doll in circle on back. Circa 1946-50. Retains excellent coloring, original box.

83. Mary Hoyer Bride with Box
14". Five-piece hard plastic body, short brown saran wig, grey sleep eyes, smoky shadow, brush lashes, face has a matte finish. Heavy white satin gown with hand beading, lace and sequin detail, matching train attaches by hook to the back and sides, open pillbox-style cap and veil, floral bouquet with ribbons, cream strap slippers. Marked Original Mary Hoyer Doll in circle on back. Circa 1946-50. Although this award-winning gown is not an original Hoyer design, it is exquisitely sewn and detailed.

84. Mary Hoyer with Box
14". Five-piece hard plastic body, blonde curled mohair wig, grey sleep eyes with smoky shadow, brush lashes. Marked Original Mary Hoyer Doll on back in circle. Circa 1946-50. Comes in original box with white snap shoes and socks.

85. Mary Hoyer with Box
14". Five-piece hard plastic body, short brunette mohair wig, green sleep eyes with smoky shadow, brush lashes. Marked Original Mary Hoyer Doll on back in circle. Circa 1946-50. Comes with black snap shoes and socks in original box with "Festival Dolls" label over the Hoyer logo.

Nancy Ann Storybook Dolls
All are 5 1/2" (unless noted) with a five-piece hard plastic body, sleep eyes and painted black slippers. They are marked Storybook Dolls USA Trade Mark Reg on their back. Circa 1948-50 with original boxes.

86. Fairytale Series "When She Was Good...." #132
Auburn wig. Blue dotted cotton gown with satin trim, nylon slip and pantalets.

87. Fairytale Series "Pretty As A Picture..." #124
Blonde wig. Multi-colored taffeta dress with purple bodice, cotton slip and panty, felt bonnet with flower.

88. Fairytale Series "Elsie Marley.." #131
Blonde wig with feather and ribbon. Red nylon dress with floral overlay panels, lace accents, cotton pantalet.

89. Seasons Series "Summer" #91
Brunette wig. Yellow satin bodice, floral nylon skirt with yellow slip, felt picture hat, pantalet. Original wrist tag.

90. Mother Goose Series "Little Red Riding Hood" #116
Brunette wig. Red polka-dotted cotton dress with lace accents, matching pantalet, red felt cape with hood.

91. Dolls Of The Day Series "Friday's Child" #184
Brunette wig with ribbon and feather. Multi-colored taffeta skirt with silver threading and trim, cotton slip and panty. She has a present in her hand and Storybook Company letter #3 in her box with special Birthday presentation front.

92. Bridal Series "Bride" #86
Auburn wig. White satin bodice, nylon skirt with overlay and lace accents, flower garland at waist, cotton skirt and pantalet, veil.

93. Operetta Series "Blossom Time" #304
6 1/2". Blonde wig. Lavender nylon (was blue) bodice with pink full nylon skirt with ribbons and flowers at waist, pantalet, blue picture straw hat. Original wrist tag and booklet.

94. Dolls Of The Day Series "Sabbath Day" #186
Brunette wig. Peach nylon bodice and skirt with ribbons and flowers at the waist, plastic lace overlay, matching hat, cotton slip and panty. Presentation box front with booklet.

95. Dolls Of The Day Series "Tuesday's Child" #181
Blonde wig with ribbons and flowers. Pink, blue and white multi-colored taffeta gown with ribbon, cotton slip and panty. Original booklet.

96. All-Time Hit Parade Series "Alice Blue Gown" #407
6 1/2". Blonde wig. Painted eyes, blue nylon gown with full tulle and lace overlays, nylon slip and pantalet, picture straw hat with flowers. Original wrist tag.

97. Madame Alexander Elise Ballerina
16″. Eleven-piece hard plastic and vinyl body, blonde wig, green sleep eyes, brush lashes, pierced ears. Tagged white satin and tulle tutu with floral garland on front, pink tights, pink vinyl ballet slippers, floral coronet, pearl earrings. Marked Alexander on head, Mme Alexander on back and has unique jointed ankles. Circa 1958. Catalogue #1735, doll retains original fresh coloring and has wrist booklet.

98. Madame Alexander Elise Ballerina with Box
16″. Eleven-piece hard plastic and vinyl body, blonde wig, green sleep eyes, brush lashes. Tagged blue satin and tulle tutu with floral garland and rhinestone accent, pink tights, pink satin ballet slippers, floral coronet. Marked Alexander on head, Mme Alexander on back and also has unique jointed ankles. Circa 1957. Doll has fresh original coloring, matte facial finish and original box marked #1635.

99. Madame Alexander Lissy Bridesmaid
11". Nine-piece hard plastic jointed body, blonde wig, green sleep eyes, molded lashes. Tagged gown of pink nylon with tulle overlay, silver threads through bodice and "pearl" neckline, satin waist ribbon, pink panty, hose, headdress of tulle and rosebuds, baby Louis heels, rhinestone bracelet and nosegay. Circa 1956. Fashion #1248.

100. Madame Alexander Lissy Bridesmaid
11". Nine-piece hard plastic jointed body, brunette wig, green sleep eyes, molded lashes. Tagged gown of pink nylon with wide val lace inserts and bodice, satin waist ribbon, separate slip and panty, tulle hat with flowers, baby Louis heels. Circa 1957. Fashion #1161.

101. Madame Alexander Brenda Starr with Box
11 1/2". Seven-piece hard plastic and vinyl body, red saran rooted hair, blue sleep eyes, molded lashes. Tagged pink cotton dress with lace hem, separate slip, pink heels. Marked Alexander 1964 on head, Alexander on back. Circa 1964. #900 with original box and booklet.

102. Madame Alexander Brenda Starr with Box
11 1/2". Seven-piece hard plastic and vinyl body, red saran rooted hair, blue sleep eyes, molded lashes. Tagged white lace teddy, white heels. Marked as above. Circa 1964. #900 with original box, booklet and stand.

Betsy McCall
All Betsy McCall dolls are 8" with a seven-piece jointed hard plastic body marked McCall Corp in a small circle on the lower back, eyes are green-grey and have molded lashes. Clothing is hard to identify for many collectors, as it is neither marked or tagged.

103. Sun 'n Sand
Tosca rooted wig, red polka dot swimsuit, fringed cotton hat, beach bag and blanket with matching multi-colored zigzag design, rhinestone sandals. Circa 1958, fashion #B43.

104. Sugar and Spice
Brunette rooted wig, pink nylon gown with flocked black dots and edging, black sleeveless bodice with pink shoulder drape, stiff net slip, panty and black side-button shoes. Circa 1958, fashion #B61.

105. Town & Country
Brunette rooted wig, dress of white bodice and sleeves with black and white checked skirt, red piping, matching coat and black beret, nylon chemise, white side-button shoes. Circa 1958, fashion #B42.

106. Riding Habit
Tosca rooted wig, one-piece outfit of red and white checked shirt with attached brown felt jodhpurs, green suedene vest, nylon head scarf, black side-button shoes. Circa 1958.

107. Betsy McCall
Red wig glued directly to head, body as described previously. Wearing nylon patterned chemise with socks and black side-button shoes. Circa 1958. Original "face box" marked B100 with a $2.25 price.

108. Betsy McCall
Blonde wig glued directly to head, body described previously. Wearing floral nylon chemise with thicker socks, black side-button shoes. Circa 1958. Original "face box" marked B100.

108A. Betsy McCall
Brunette wig rooted into cap, body as described previously. Wears nylon chemise with rosebud print, thick socks, white side-button shoes. Circa 1958. Early starburst box stamped B100/225 and B7 written on end, includes original booklet and original Newberry's price tag on bottom.

109. Betsy McCall Fashion
Outfit #B4 "Ballerina" with red nylon and tulle tutu, panty, ballet slippers and bouquet in original box.

110. Betsy McCall Fashion
Outfit #B23 "Brunch Time" with pink gingham pajamas, quilted white robe with matching piping, socks and white side-button shoes in original box.

111. Madame Alexander Cinderella

21″. Five-piece hard plastic body, blonde floss wig braided across top of head, blue-green sleep eyes, brush lashes, ruby lips. Tagged white satin gown with side panniers, silver braided trim and scattered silver star accents, attached full slip, panty, hose and silver shoes. Accessories include silver bead bracelet and necklace, golden braided tiara and gold mesh hair snood. Circa 1948-49. Hard-to-find size for this exquisite doll with fresh and vivid coloring, similar in characteristics to the rarer portrait series of the same time.

112. *American Character Sweet Sue Formal*

18". Five-piece hard plastic walker body, light brown saran wig, green sleep eyes, brush lashes. Pink nylon gown with lace and tulle layers, floral and ribbon accents, matching slip and panty, wide open picture hat, cream center-snap shoes. Circa 1953.

113. *Arranbee Nanette Formal*

18". Five-piece hard plastic walker body, brunette saran wig with flowers, blue sleep eyes, brush lashes. Purple gown with flocked pastel design and flowers, silver trim at neckline crosses in back and is attached to gown at wrists, large purple satin bow at back, attached double slip with hoop, panty, silver slippers. Marked R&B on head. Circa 1953-55. Has original wrist booklet.

114. *Madame Alexander Southern Belle*
8". Hard plastic bent-knee walker body, uniquely-curled wig, green sleep eyes, molded lashes. Tagged aqua and white striped gown with flared sleeves, overskirt, large back bustle and train, cotton full slip and pantaloons, black straw hat with flowers and fruit, black side-snap shoes. Marked Alex on back. Circa 1956. A hard-to-find doll with exquisite outfit detail.

115. *Madame Alexander Victoria*
8". Five-piece walker body, curled light brown wig, green sleep eyes, molded lashes. Tagged slate-blue taffeta gown with side pannier and bustle drapery, elaborate trim, net half-sleeves, full slip, eyelet pantaloons, lace floral cap, satin reticule, cream side-snap shoes. Marked Alex on back. Circa 1954. #0030C from the "Me and My Shadow" Series.

116. *Madame Alexander Nana Wendy's Governess*
8". Seven-piece hard plastic bent-knee walker body, auburn curled wig, black sleep eyes, molded lashes. Tagged pink and white striped shirt, black velvet skirt with attached rhinestone buckle, cotton full slip and pantaloons, black straw hat with net and flowers, black trimmed faux purse, black side-snap shoes. Marked Alex on back. Circa 1957. #433 with original hanging price tag.

117. Madame Alexander Scarlett

8". Five-piece hard plastic walker body, brown curled wig, grey sleep eyes, molded lashes. Tagged chintz floral-print, multi-layered dress with green piping and bows, tulle sleeves and neckline, full cotton slip, pantaloons, straw picture hat with flowers, black side-snap shoes. Marked Alex on back. Circa 1955. #485 Scarlett in earlier gown.

118. Madame Alexander Cousin Grace

8". Seven-piece hard plastic bent-knee walker body, auburn curled wig, black sleep eyes, molded lashes. Tagged blue organdy gown with floral print, lace ruffled accents with occasional flowers, large back bow, taffeta slip with tulle, matching panty, straw picture hat with flowers, choker with rhinestone, blue side-snap shoes. Marked Alex on back. Circa 1957. #432 from the Gone with the Wind series.

119. Madame Alexander Country Picnic

8". Five-piece hard plastic walker body, blonde wig, grey sleep eyes, molded lashes. Tagged white jacket with lace edging over pink and white gingham dress with ric-rac trim, full cotton slip with matching pantaloon, black straw hat with flowers, black side-snap shoes. Marked Alex on back. Circa 1953. #376 Country Picnic outfit.

120. Terri Lee with Trunk and Clothing

15 1/2". Five-piece hard plastic body, wiry brunette wig with two braids at top going down back of hair (molded hair underneath), painted brown eyes with lashes, eyebrows and full red mouth. White sleeveless blouse, red wool jacket, plaid kilt and cap, cotton panty, green felt shoulder bag, white tie shoes. Marked Terri Lee Pat. Pending on back. Circa 1948, wearing Scotch outfit #140. Early version of the doll rarer hairstyle and original daisy wrapped around her wrist. Travel trunk includes many tagged pieces of Terri Lee clothing and accessories, original yellow wrist booklet.

121. Mary Jane Walker

16". Five-piece hard plastic walker body, long black wig, green sleep/flirty eyes, molded lashes. Plaid dress with white lace collar, ruffled hem, nylon panty, black snap-front shoes (also includes a red coat). Unmarked. Circa 1953. Kathryn Kay Fassel was an employee of the Terri Lee Company for a short period. She then left, and returning to the East Coast, began manufacturing this doll in conjunction with the GH & E Freydberg Inc company. The doll seriously encroached on Terri Lee's sales and in 1954 was ordered to be withdrawn from the market due to a patent infringement lawsuit.

122. Jerri Lee with Box

16". Five-piece hard plastic body, light blonde sheepskin wig, painted brown eyes and lashes, full pink mouth. Tagged red satin band jacket with gold trim accents, white satin pants, red blocked hat, white boots with red cut-out accents. Marked Terri Lee on back. Circa 1948-52, wearing #2082 Drum Major Costume. Includes box (tagged for Terri Lee-original price tag $14.95) and Fashion Parade booklet from earlier period in Lincoln, Nebraska.

123. Terri Lee "Bonnie Lou"
16". Five-piece brown hard plastic body, black curled soft wig with red ribbons, painted brown eyes with unusual sweeping eye lashes, full pink mouth. Tagged plaid dress with white collar and front, cotton undershirt and panty, red and white shoes. Marked Terri Lee on head and back. Circa 1947. Harder-to-find model in exceptional condition with original daisy on wrist.

39

124. Vogue Kindergarten Ginny
7 1/2". Five-piece hard plastic body, light brown long wig with flowers and ribbons, brown sleep eyes, painted lashes. Red velvet bodice with flowers, polka dot taffeta skirt with matching panty, red center-snap shoes. Marked Vogue Doll on back. Circa 1951. #32 Nan from the Kindergarten Series.

125. Vogue Tiny Miss Ginny
7 1/2". Five-piece hard plastic body, light brown braided wig, blue sleep eyes, painted lashes. Tagged plaid taffeta dress with organdy trim and hem, red piping, matching panty, stiff slip, straw hat with cherries, red center-snap shoes. Marked Vogue Doll on back. Circa 1952. #42 Tiny Miss Series with original wrist tag.

126. Vogue Pixie
7 1/2". Five-piece hard plastic body, red caracul wig, red hairbow, blue sleep eyes, painted lashes. Tagged red and white organdy dress with stitched floral trim accents, matching panty, red center-snap shoes. Marked Vogue Doll on back. Circa 1952, the only year dolls with this sheepskin "Pixie" hairdo were offered.

127. Vogue Beach Ginny
8". Five-piece hard plastic walker body, blonde braided wig, blue sleep eyes, painted lashes. Tagged blue knit swimsuit outfit with terry cover-up and matching hat, blue tie shoes. Marked Ginny Vogue Dolls Inc Pat Pend Made in USA. Circa 1953, #48 Beach from the Gadabout Series. Includes a bonus pair of swim fins and mask, original wrist tag, stand and rare Freddie the Fish inflatable swim accessory.

128. Vogue Kindergarten Ginny

8″. Five-piece hard plastic body, blonde curled wig with large green bow, blue sleep eyes, painted lashes. Tagged dress of satin faux lace print bottom with petal-shaped velvet overlay and bodice, matching satin panty, white tie shoes. Marked Vogue Doll on back. Circa 1952. #30 Kindergarten Series "Dawn" with original metal Vogue stand.

129. Vogue Kindergarten Ginny

8″. Five-piece hard plastic body, red braided wig with yellow ribbons, blue sleep eyes, painted lashes. Tagged brown and white checked dress with yellow/green ric-rac tape trim, matching panty, tan socks, black center-snap shoes. Marked Vogue Doll on back. Circa 1953. #29 Kindergarten School Series "Tina".

130. Vogue Kinder Crowd Ginny

8″. Five-piece hard plastic walker body, red curled wig with green bow, blue sleep eyes, painted lashes. Tagged green taffeta dress with velvet ribbon and flower trim, matching panty, green vinyl shoes. Marked Ginny Vogue Dolls Inc Pat Pend Made in USA on back. Circa 1954. #25 My Kinder Crowd Series, includes original cardboard circle wrist tag.

131. Vogue "Gretel" Ginny

8″. Five-piece hard plastic body, yellow braided wig, brown sleep eyes, painted lashes. Tagged storybook outfit of printed organdy with multi-colored satin ribbon and lace trim, matching panty, straw hat, green center-snap shoes. Marked Vogue Doll on back. Circa 1953. #34 Gretel from the Twin Series. Although this particular hat is not documented, it may be original as this doll came from the original owner to whom it was given as a gift.

132. Vogue "Hansel" Ginny

8″. Five-piece hard plastic body, blonde page-boy cut wig, blue sleep eyes, painted lashes. One-piece outfit of organdy shirt with attached cerise suedene shorts with rosebuds at sides, and satin "suspenders" and waist, cap with flowers and feather, green shoes. Marked Vogue Doll on back. Circa 1953. #33 Hansel from the Twin Series.

Left to Right/Top to Bottom:
Madame Alexander Cissette

All 10" Cissettes have a seven-piece hard plastic adult body with grey sleep eyes, molded lashes, brightly colored lips, painted fingernails, tagged lace teddies (except Margot) pearl drop earrings, gold open-toe heels and are marked Mme Alexander on their backs. They debuted in 1957 and were miniature models for the top fashions of the day. All include original boxes and are catalogue #700. Circa 1957-62.

133. Blonde wig, wrist booklet and original I. Magnin price tag ($3.00).

134. Brunette wig, hose, straw hat, wrist booklet.

135. Tosca wig, wrist booklet, I. Magnin price tag ($3.00).

136. Margot with brunette upswept wig, blue eyeshadow, enhanced lashes. Wears floral ribbon bandeau, purple suedene wrap short, hose and black heels. Has "Portrait" wrist booklet. Circa 1961-63.

137. Auburn wig, plain nails, wrist booklet, I. Magnin price tag ($3.00).

138. Blonde wig, tagged black velvet-type dress with sequined neckline, full pink slip with net, pink panty, hose, white stole, rhinestone earrings, silver heels. Fashion #973, circa 1957.

139. Brunette wig, black velvet fitted dress with dotted tulle overlay, flowers at waist, hose, pearl necklace, rhinestone glued to finger, brown mink stole and muff, black heels. Fashion #974 Dressed for the Theatre, circa 1957.

140. Blonde wigged Margot, lilac satin gown with sequined neckline and straps, stiff pink full slip, hose, hair bow, necklace, rhinestone glued to finger and gold heels. She wears her original halter outfit with black wrap short underneath. Fashion #920, circa 1961.

141. Brunette wig Jacqueline with rhinestone metal accent, tagged pink satin evening gown with waist bow, full pink slip, panty, hose, bead necklace, rhinestone on finger, beaded purse, gold heels and wrist booklet in original box marked #885, circa 1962.

141A. Blonde wig, tagged dotted tulle gown with flowers and satin waist ribbon, pink full slip, hose, panty, horsehair braid picture hat with flowers, silver heels. Circa 1957. Fashion #960 Bridesmaid with box.

Left to Right/Top to Bottom

Ideal Toni dolls are all five-piece hard plastic bodies with green/grey sleep eyes and brush lashes. Clothing varied but use this picture as an example of how many different variations there can be of one style or outfit. The dress here is varied five different ways. Circa 1951.

142. 14″. Blonde wig, pink shirt with attached aqua and gold skirt, panty, white vinyl shoes. Marked Ideal Doll P-90 head and back.

143. 19″. Blonde wig, tagged pink waffle weave shirt with attached green and gold skirt, matching purse, cotton slip and panty, gold center-snap shoes. Marked Ideal Doll P-92 Made in USA on head and Ideal Doll P-19 on back. Harder-to-find large size with complete outfit.

144. 14". Auburn wig, pink shirt with attached aqua and gold skirt, cotton slip and panty, white vinyl shoes. Marked Ideal Doll P-90 on head and back. Original box, hang tag (with #1140) and Play Wave set. Doll has exceptionally high color and harder-to-find red hair color.

145. 16". Brunette wig, tagged pink shirt with attached green and gold skirt, cotton slip and panty, white tie shoes. Marked Ideal Doll P-91 on head and back.

146. 14". Dark brunette wig, tagged waffle weave pink shirt with attached blue and gold skirt, cotton slip, nylon panty, white vinyl shoes. Marked Ideal Doll P-90 on head and back.

147. *Arranbee Cinderella*
14". Five-piece hard plastic body, blonde upswept floss wig with flowers, blue sleep eyes, brush lashes. Pink nylon and satin gown with panniers, silver braid trimming, flowers, glitter stars and attached satin slip with insert to straighten gown front, matching panty, thigh hose and clear "glass" slippers. Unmarked. Circa 1952. Hard-to-find character in exceptional condition.

Muffie Playtime Dolls by Nancy Ann

Muffie was introduced around 1953 and soon rose to compete with Vogue's Ginny. The early doll has a five-piece hard plastic body (marked Storybook Dolls California) with a Saran wig that had many different styles. All dolls below have sleep eyes and painted lashes but facial characteristics varied as some had no eyebrows, while others had painted lashes and molded lashes together. They have the original boxes with #500 and original May Co price sticker ($1.00).

148. Brunette Muffie wearing pink nylon panty, white shoes.

149. Blonde Muffie wearing white cotton panty, red shoes.

150. Red-headed Muffie wearing blue nylon panty, white shoes.

151. Strawberry-blonde Muffie wearing pink formal dress with lace and floral trim, pink panty and shoes, carries original purse.

152. Monica Dolls "Marion"
14". Hard plastic five-piece body, rooted dark blonde human hair, green sleep eyes, brush lashes, red mouth. Wears blue nylon formal gown with gathered princess waist, chiffon petal neckline and straps with trimmed rosebuds, cream tie slippers with glitter dot, flower petal earrings. Marked Made in U.S.A. on back. Circa 1949. One of the last dolls produced by the Monica Studios who was primarily known for their composition namesake. A rare doll having the rooted hair trademark of the firm was produced in two sizes, 18" and the harder-to-find 14" model as portrayed here. Very few examples are known to exist.

153. Madame Alexander Cissy Formal

20". Nine-piece hard plastic and vinyl body, light brown curled upswept wig, green sleep eyes, brush lashes. Tagged pink taffeta torso gown with gathered neckline and sweeping diagonal side drapery with rhinestone ornaments, long full slip, panty, hose, silver heels, rhinestone and pearl earrings. Circa 1956. Fashion #2036.

154. *Madame Alexander Cissy Bridesmaid*
20″. Nine-piece hard plastic and vinyl body, blonde wig, green sleep eyes, brush lashes. Tagged blue formal gown of nylon with pleated tulle overlay skirt and cap sleeves, silver-threaded net bodice with "pearl" neckline, rhinestone accents, satin waist ribbon, nylon panty, hose, tulle headpiece with flowers, floral bouquet, blue engagement ring, silver heels. Circa 1956. Fashion #2030 Bridesmaid.

155. *Madame Alexander Cissy Formal*
20″. Nine-piece hard plastic and vinyl body, blonde styled wig, green sleep eyes, brush lashes. Tagged black velvet gown with ornamental braid at neckline, long full slip, panty, hose, fur stole, drop earrings, pearl necklace, rhinestone bracelet, engagement ring and black heels complete this ensemble. Marked Alexander on head. Circa 1957. Fashion #2173.

156. Madame Alexander Cissy
20". Nine-piece hard plastic and vinyl body, brunette wig, blue sleep eyes, brush lashes. Tagged aqua taffeta cocktail dress with black velvet bolero jacket with corsage, pink nylon full slip and panty, hose, silver heels, floral and net headpiece. Circa 1957. Fashion #2017 with original box.

157. Madame Alexander Cissy
20". Seven-piece hard plastic and vinyl body, blonde wig, blue/green sleep eyes, brush lashes. Nylon lace blouse with rhinestone buttons, pink silk side sash with beaded accent, black velvet pants, pearl drop earrings, black heels. Marked Alexander on head. Circa 1957. Extra stock fashion outfit for Cissy.

158. Cosmopolitan Ginger
8". Five-piece hard plastic body, blonde Saran wig, blue sleep eyes, molded lashes. Tagged green nylon dress with pink trim and attached slip, panty, pink vinyl shoes. Circa 1955. With original stand and box (labelled #334) for the dress she wears.

159. Cosmopolitan Ginger
8". Five-piece hard plastic walker body, blonde saran wig, blue sleep eyes, molded lashes. Tagged blue nylon dress with flocked dots, lace trim, panty, straw hat, blue vinyl shoes. Circa 1955.

Ginger Fashions in Original Boxes

160. Tagged blue nylon dress with tulle and attached silver glitter wings, crown, wand, sequin band, panty, tie shoes and Ginger Doll-er in box marked #1012 Oct. 1957.

161. Tagged blue gingham long dress with eyelet trim, matching bonnet, organdy apron and cotton pantaloon. Box marked #1008.

162. White and green satin Carmen Miranda-style outfit of white with green ruffled bodysuit with matching wrap-around skirt, hat with fruit and green tie shoes. Box marked #1007.

163. Tagged red velvet and dotted tulle formal dress, straw picture hat, hankie, purse and tie shoes. Includes Baby Ginger booklet and comes in brown "Doll Dress Of The Month Club" box marked #776-293 Feb 1956.

164. Tagged red cotton shirt, fur print vest and chaps, yellow scarf, gun belt, cowboy hat and boots. Box marked #664.

165. Arranbee Nanette with Box
20". Five-piece hard plastic walking body, blonde Saran wig, blue/green sleep eyes. Aqua herringbone weave cotton dress with unusual pleated trim and fruit cluster accents, stiff cotton slip, panty, black snap shoes. Marked R&B on head. Circa 1955. Exquisite doll in hard-to-find larger size retaining fresh, original coloring with her box.

166. Vogue Jill with Box
10". Seven-piece hard plastic walker body, blonde Saran wig, blue sleep eyes, molded lashes. Lingerie set of bra and girdle, pearl heart earrings, white heels. Marked "Jill Vogue Doll Inc Made in USA c 1957" on back. Circa 1957. Original box with #3013 (Haircut is called Angel Cut) and wrist tag.

167. Vogue Jan in Box
10". Six-piece hard vinyl body (swivel-waist), rooted brunette hair, green sleep eyes, molded lashes. Lingerie panty girdle and bra, hose, pearl heart earrings, white heels. Marked Vogue on head. Circa 1958. Harder-to-find Jan with original box.

168. Vogue Jeff
10". Five-piece hard vinyl body, molded black hair, grey sleep eyes, molded lashes. Two-piece aqua cowboy outfit with black inserts and silver fringe accents, plastic guns and holster, black boots. Marked Vogue Dolls on back. Circa 1958. Original Vogue stand. Outfit #6461.

169. Vogue Jill
10". Seven-piece hard plastic body, blonde wig with headband and original butterfly hairpin, blue sleep eyes, molded lashes. Tagged pink nylon strapless dress with flocked floral design, lace and satin accents, slip and panty, hose, pearl necklace and drop earrings, pink heels. Marked Vogue on head and "Jill Vogue Dolls Inc Made in USA © 1957" on back. Outfit #3140 with original metal Jill doll stand.

170. Ideal Toni with Box
14″. Five-piece hard plastic body, brunette wig, green sleep eyes, brush lashes. Tagged blue plaid dress with organdy blouse, attached cotton slip, panty, white snap-front shoes. Marked P-90 Ideal Doll Made in USA on head, Ideal Doll P-90 on back. Circa 1949. In original large box with Play Wave kit.

171. Ideal Toni with Box
14″. Five-piece hard plastic body, red wig, green sleep eyes, brush lashes. Tagged red dress with yellow ric-rac trim, organdy top, attached slip, white snap-front shoes. Marked as above on head and body. Circa 1950. Has top of original box only.

172. Ideal Toni with Box
15″. Five-piece hard plastic body, red nylon wig, blue sleep eyes, brush lashes. Tagged cotton dress with grey and salmon multi-print, organdy pinafore with matching trim, attached cotton slip and panty, white vinyl shoes. Marked P-91 Ideal Doll Made in USA on head, Ideal Doll P-91 on back. Circa 1950. Has original wrist tags, Play Wave kit and box marked #1160. Beautiful and vivid color combination of eyes, dress and hair.

173. *Vogue Formal Ginny*
8". Seven-piece bent-knee hard plastic walker body, blonde ponytail wig, blue sleep eyes, molded lashes. Tagged pink nylon formal with embroidered trim, satin ribbons, panty, horsehair picture hat, white vinyl shoes. Marked Vogue on head and Ginny Vogue Dolls Inc Pat No 2687594 Made in USA on back. Circa 1957. Fashion #7172, with doll #7072.

174. *Vogue Tiny Miss Ginny*
8". Five-piece hard plastic body, blonde wig, brown sleep eyes, painted lashes. Tagged blue taffeta dress with floral garland, silver threading, panty, straw hat with matching flowers, purse, blue snap shoes. Marked Vogue Doll on back. Circa 1953. #44 "Cheryl" from the Tiny Miss Series.

175. *Vogue Ginny*
8". Five-piece hard plastic body, blonde braided wig, blue sleep eyes, painted lashes. Tagged red gingham shirt with zipper, denim jeans, straw hat, glasses, red snap shoes. Marked Vogue Doll on back. Circa 1953. #70 "A.M." from the Talon Zipper Fashions.

176. *Vogue Tennis Ginny*
8". Five-piece hard plastic walker body, red braided wig, brown sleep eyes, painted lashes. Tagged white cotton tennis dress with matching panty, green knit sweater and cap with racquet design, glasses, plastic racquet, white vinyl shoes. Marked Ginny Vogue Dolls Inc Pat Pend Made in USA on back. Circa 1954. #46 For Fun Time series with original box.

177. *Vogue Gym Kids Ginny*
8". Five-piece hard plastic walker body, blonde braided wig, blue eyes, molded lashes. Tagged pink and grey print shirt, jeans with matching cuffs, vinyl cap, black vinyl shoes. Marked with 2687594 patent number on back. Circa 1956. #6027 Gym Kids Fashion.

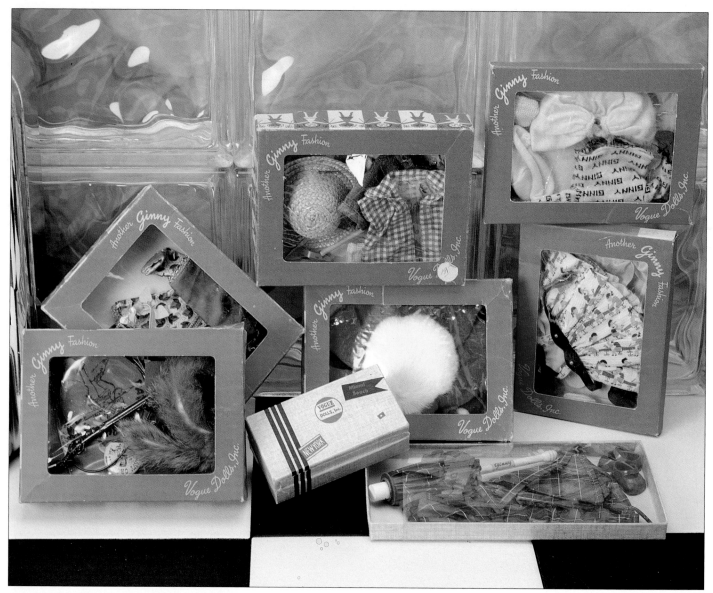

Boxed Ginny Fashions and Accessories
Top to Bottom/Right to Left

178. Tagged red gingham top with zipper, jeans, straw hat, metal and wooden rake, red vinyl shoes. Circa 1954, #670.

179. Yellow knit pullover with black Ginny name, yellow skirt with attached panty (has unusual pink lining), matching cap, yellow socks, black vinyl shoes. Circa 1955, #130.

180. Tagged floral print top with zipper, green pants, gold flower headband, belt and glasses, bead bracelet, gold shoes. Circa 1955, #53 And Away We Go Series.

181. Tagged red velvet coat with pom-poms, fur cap and muff, white vinyl shoes. Circa 1955, #183.

182. Tagged yellow dress with multi-print skirt, black patent belt, yellow hairbow, yellow socks, black vinyl shoes. Circa 1955.

183. Tan two-piece suedene "fringed" jacket and pants, tagged fur "coonskin" cap, brown metal rifle, belt, Davy Crockett patch and button. Circa 1955.

184. Tagged aqua and gold skating outfit with matching cap, panty and roller skates in suitcase. Circa 1955.

185. Red plaid vinyl raincape with Ginny on visor, matching umbrella and red vinyl shoes. Circa 1959.

186. Arranbee Nancy Lee
17". Five-piece hard plastic body, brownish floss wig, blue/green sleep eyes, brush lashes. Red dotted organdy dress with apron and sleeve accents, panty, red straw hat, white snap shoes. Circa 1950. Early model with excellent coloring.

187. Arranbee Nanette
17". Five-piece hard plastic body, golden wig, blue/green sleep eyes, brush lashes. Pink nylon dress with floral print, attached flowers and wrist ribbon, slip and panty, straw basket, pearl necklace, faux wrist watch and pink snap shoes. Circa 1950, has original wrist tag and vivid original coloring.

188. Ideal Little Miss Revlon with Case
10 1/2″. Six-piece hard vinyl body, blonde rooted wig, green sleep eyes, molded lashes, painted nails. Tagged blue cotton and flocked organdy dress, nylon slip and panty, hose, necklace and earrings, red purse and heels, white straw hat and original wrist booklet. The case contains assorted clothing, accessories and booklet. Marked Ideal Doll 10 1/2 on head. Circa 1958-60. Hard-to-find case and high coloring to the doll.

189. Arranbee Coty Girl with Box
10 1/2″. Six-piece hard vinyl body, tosca rooted wig, green sleep eyes, molded lashes, painted nails. White and gold strapless gown, panty, hose, pearl earrings, gold open-toe heels with a rhinestone, green straw hat. Marked 10 1/2R under right arm. Circa 1958. Original box.

190. Ideal Little Miss Revlon with Box
10 1/2". Six-piece hard vinyl body, rooted brunette wig, green sleep eyes, molded lashes, painted nails. Lacy lingerie bra and girdle, pearl earrings, pink heels. Marked Ideal Doll VT-10 1/2 on head. Circa 1958-60. With original box ($2.98 price).

191. Ideal Sara Ann
15". Five-piece hard plastic body, dark blonde wig, blue sleep eyes, brush lashes. Green cotton dress with striped collar and sleeves, cotton slip and panty, green shoulder bag with curlers, tan bag with plastic wraps, white vinyl shoes. Marked P-90 Ideal Doll on head and back. Circa 1951. Original wrist tag.

192. Ideal Toni
20". Five-piece hard plastic body, curled platinum blonde wig, green sleep eyes, brush lashes. Green cotton dress with attached panty, pink organdy pinafore, pink vinyl shoes. Marked P-93 Ideal Doll on head and back. Circa 1950. Larger size with exceptional long and curly wig.

193. Ideal Toni
16". Five-piece hard plastic body, light blonde wig, blue sleep eyes, brush lashes. Tagged cotton print dress with attached panty, organdy pinafore with ric-rac trim, white vinyl shoes. Marked Ideal Doll P-91 on head and back. Circa 1950. Fresh original coloring.

194. Madame Alexander Queen Elizabeth

8″. Five-piece hard plastic walker body, light brown wig, grey sleep eyes, molded lashes. Tagged cream taffeta gown with blue ribbon and Order of the Garter sash, red velvet robe, full slip, panty, rhinestone crown, gold tie shoes. Marked Alex on back. Circa 1955, #499.

195. Madame Alexander "Amy" with Box

8″. Seven-piece bent-knee walker body, blonde wig in special style, grey sleep eyes, molded lashes. Tagged floral print aqua dress with lace inset and collar, full cotton slip and pantalet, black side-snap shoes. Marked Alex on back. Circa 1958. Original box labelled "Kins 581 Amy".

196. Madame Alexander Formal

8″. Five-piece hard plastic body, blonde upswept wig with ribbon, grey sleep eyes, molded lashes. Formal white organdy dress with red ric-rac trim atop ruffles, satin ribbon, lacy slip, panty, red reticule, cream snap shoes. Marked Alex on back. Circa 1955. #476 Wendy Loves to Waltz outfit.

197. Madame Alexander Flower Girl
8". Seven-piece hard plastic walker body, blonde hair atop head with flowers, black sleep eyes, molded lashes. Tagged white satin gown with lace accents, pink stripe ribbon sash with pearl buckle, full net slip, panty, cream tie shoes, bouquet. Circa 1956. Original box for #602 Flower Girl.

198. Madame Alexander Maggie Mixup Walker
8". Seven-piece hard plastic walker body, red wig, green sleep eyes, molded lashes, freckles. Tagged blue cotton jumper over striped unitard, carries red purse, black shoes. Marked Alex on back. Circa 1960.

199. Madame Alexander Billy
8". Seven-piece hard plastic walker body, blonde styled wig, grey sleep eyes, molded lashes. Tagged white knit bodysuit with star at neck, blue striped shorts, cream tie shoes. Marked Alex on back. Circa 1960. In box labelled #300.

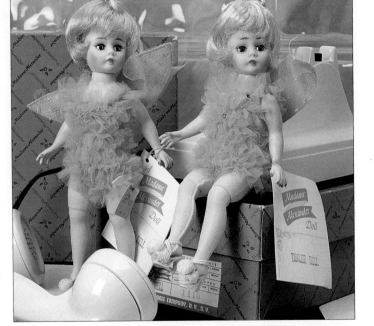

200. Madame Alexander Maggie Mixup Walker
8". Seven-piece hard plastic walker body, red wig, green sleep eyes, molded lashes, freckles and smile. Tagged outfit as described in #198 but with blue purse. Marked Alex on back. Circa 1960.

201. Madame Alexander Tinker Bell with Box
10". Seven-piece hard plastic adult body, blonde styled short wig, grey eyes with blue shadow, molded lashes, painted side lashes, painted fingernails. Tagged pink ruffled tulle leotard with rhinestone accents, silver threaded wings, hose, pink pompom heels. Circa 1969. #1110 with original wrist booklet and box.

202. Madame Alexander Tinker Bell with Box
10". Same features as described above but having original Disneyland tag ($12.95) and rectangular box. Circa 1969-72. #1110 with rectangular box.

Madame Alexander Cissettes

All Cissettes are 10" dolls with seven-piece hard plastic bodies marked Mme Alexander on back with grey sleep eyes and molded lashes. Circa 1958-60.

203. Tosca wig, tagged pink polished cotton dress with rhinestone accents, lace ruffles, stiff slip, satin panty, straw bonnet with flowers, silver heels, with original box and booklet. Fashion #813 variation.

204. Blonde wig, tagged pink polished cotton dress similar to above, nylon slip & panty, hose, straw bonnet, purse, silver heels. Fashion #813.

205. Auburn wig, red polished cotton dress with lace neckline, tagged pink full slip and panty, hose, tagged white vinyl overcoat, purse, straw hat, red heels. Outfit #913 (dress).

206. Blonde wig, red cotton apron-front dress with attached organdy blouse, slip, panty, hose, rhinestone earrings, red shoes. Fashion #810 in box.

207. Blonde wig, yellow striped sun outfit of a bathing suit with tie around skirt, yellow sun hat, pearl earrings, glasses, hose and white heels. Outfit #805.

208. Brunette wig, tagged multi-colored nehru-style jacket, yellow pants, white heels.

209. Renoir Portrette
Brunette long curled wig, blue eyeshadow, tagged blue taffeta gown with lace, flowers and pleated ruffles, stiff net slip, panty, blue straw hat with flowers and tulle, hose, blue heels. Circa 1970, #1180.

210. Godey Portrette
Red long curled wig, blue eyeshadow, tagged yellow taffeta gown with ruffled layers, lace overlay and bows, long stiff net slip, panty, straw hat with tulle, gold heels. Circa 1969, #1175.

211. Cissette Ballerina
Tosca wig, tagged gold ballet tutu with flecked net and sequins, matching headpiece, tights, gold ballet slippers. Circa 1959. #713, made for one year only, comes with Cissette box.

212. Wendy Ballerina
8". Seven-piece hard plastic walker body, tosca wig, grey sleep eyes, molded lashes. Tagged blue satin tutu with tulle overlay, rhinestones and flowers, tights, floral garland, pink ballet slippers. Circa 1957.

213. Madame Alexander Elise Ballerina with Box
16″. Eleven-piece hard plastic and vinyl body with jointed ankles, red wig with curl across top of head behind floral headpiece, blue sleep eyes, brush lashes. Tagged yellow satin and tulle tutu with floral garland and rhinestone accents, pink tights, satin ballet slippers. Marked Alexander on head and Mme Alexander on back. Circa 1957. #1635 with original box in hard-to-find yellow tutu, exceptional coloring.

214. Madame Alexander Winnie Walker
15″. Five-piece hard plastic walker body, blonde curled wig, blue sleep eyes, brush lashes. Tagged pink polished cotton pinafore-styled dress with blue print sleeves, collar and back, ric-rac trim, full cotton slip and panty, pink felt hat with matching strings, black snap shoes. Marked Alexander on head. Circa 1954, the first year this doll was introduced.

215. Madame Alexander Winnie Walker
15″. Body as described above. Tagged outfit of red taffeta dress with matching panty, grey cloth coat with large white collar, red felt hat, snap shoes. Circa 1954. Fashion #1536 with original hatbox containing curlers.

216. Remco Littlechap Family
Set of four various-sized dolls all having five-piece hard vinyl bodies, rooted hair for women, molded hair for men, with painted facial features. They come dressed in tagged, original terrycloth bath attire. Marked on lower back (in circle) with name of doll Remco Industries 1963. Circa 1963. Includes Dr. John, wife Lisa, and daughters Judy and Libby in original boxes with assorted stands and one fashion booklet.

217. Hasbro GI Joe
11 1/2". Sixteen-piece hard plastic body, blonde flocked hair and beard, painted facial features including cheek scar, brown eyes. Tagged grey flight suit with shoulder gun holster, boots and plastic dog tag. Marked GI JOE copyright 1964 BY HASBRO PAT NO 3277602 Made in USA on buttocks. Circa 1970. #7403 Air Adventurer in original box.

218. Hasbro GI Joe
11 1/2". Body as described above, brown flocked hair only, blue painted eyes. Tagged two-piece green military uniform, boots and metal dog tag. Marked as above. Circa 1970. #7500 Man of Action in original box with boot removal instructions.

219. Ideal Tammy with Box
12". Five-piece hard plastic and vinyl body, rooted auburn short hair, painted blue eyes. Wears blue and white gym suit, vinyl sneakers. Marked Ideal Toy Co BS-12/1 on head and back. Circa 1962. #9000-1 with original box, fashion booklet, stand and tennis racquet. Tammy was Ideal's version of a typical teen-ager with a more realistic figure than Barbie's. Her outfits, especially accessories, rival Barbie's, as well.

220. Ideal Tammy's Parents
12 1/2 and 13". Both have bodies as described above, father has brown eyes and molded hair, mother has rooted blonde upswept wig and blue eyes with shadow. Tagged clothing as shown. Marked Ideal Toy Corp M-13/2 on Dad, W-13/L on Mom. Circa 1962. The All-American family also included a brother and little sister.

221. Tammy Family Fashions
Three Packaged fashions include #9415-1-100 for Mom, #9478-9 for Dad or Ted and Tammy accessory pak with typewriter, phone, directory and date book. Circa 1963.

222. Ideal Patty Duke Teen Doll
12". Five-piece vinyl body with poseable arms and legs, rooted light brown hair with bow, painted blue eyes. Two-piece outfit of red top with white collar, cuffs, fringe and gold star pin, grey capri pants, red shoes. Marked H on back of head. Circa 1965. Ideal #49 N 3881, star of the Patty Duke TV show with ever-present telephone in hand. Hard-to-find doll in excellent condition.

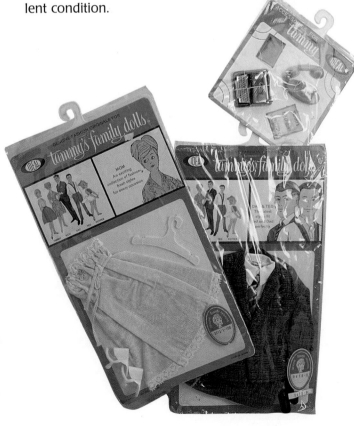

223. Ideal Tammy
Three models of the 12″ teen-ager with assorted hair colors/styles and variations to the original gym suit. All marked Ideal Toy Corp BS-12 on head. Circa 1962.

224. Ideal Pepper
Three models of the 9″ little sister of Tammy with assorted hair colors/styles and play dress variations. Marked Ideal Toy Corp 69-E on head. One has later, bendable style arms and legs. Circa 1963.

225. Ideal Shirley Temple
15″. Five-piece hard vinyl body, rooted light brown curled wig with red bow, hazel sleep eyes, brush lashes, open mouth with teeth. Tagged two-piece navy cotton sailor suit with matching hat, red ribbon tie, name pin, socks and white vinyl shoes. Marked ST-15-N on head. Circa 1960. Captain January outfit.

226. Ideal Shirley Temple
12″. Same doll as described above but with molded lashes. Marked ST-12 on head. Tagged variation of the above outfit but with black slip-on shoes. Circa 1960.

227. Packaged Shirley Temple Items
Shirley Temple Hair Styler by Gabriel includes creme rinse, dry shampoo, hair dressing and comb and Ideal Shirley Temple Fashion #9775 for a 15″ doll.

Ideal Shirley Temples

All dolls have five-piece hard vinyl bodies with light brown curled wigs, hazel sleep eyes, brush or molded lashes, open mouths with teeth. Circa 1957-60.

228. 17″. Tyrolean outfit with green felt "vest", apron and print skirt, felt cap, white vinyl shoes, name pin, flat black purse. Heidi outfit, with original box.

229. 12″. Tan jacket over tagged plaid kilt, matching hat, panty, black slip-on shoes, name pin. Wee Willie Winkie outfit.

230. 12″. Tagged organdy and print dress with attached slip, panty, name pin, straw hat, white purse, black slip-on shoes.

231. 12″. Tagged dress similar to the previous one, pink slip with neck tie and panty, black shoes. With original picture box.

232. Madame Alexander Cowgirl
8″. Seven-piece hard plastic bent-knee body, blonde wig, grey sleep eyes, molded lashes. Tagged outfit of tan suedene fringed skirt and vest with felt flowers, rhinestones and trim, attached blouse, panty, brown boots and hat. Marked Alex on back. Circa 1966-1970. #724 with original box.

233. Madame Alexander Pocahontas
8″. Brown seven-piece hard plastic body, brunette braided wig, black sleep eyes, molded lashes. Tagged brown fringed outfit with trim, beaded necklace, headband with feather, brown baby in papoose, tan slippers. Marked Alex on back. Circa 1967-70. #721 in original box with wrist tag.

234. Madame Alexander Amanda
8″. Seven-piece hard plastic walker body, red curled wig in pigtails, grey sleep eyes, molded lashes. Orange full dress with ruffled hem and sleeves, slip and pantalets, striped hose, black hat with flowers, black side-snap shoes. Marked Alex on back. Circa 1961. #489 Amanda from the Americana Series.

235. Madame Alexander American Girl with Box
8″. Seven-piece hard plastic walker body, blonde braided wig, grey sleep eyes, molded lashes. Tagged red gingham dress with eyelet pinafore, slip with net, pantalets, white knit hose, straw hat with flowers, black slippers. Marked Alex on back. Circa 1962. #388 American Girl with original box.

236. Madame Alexander Faith
8″. Seven-piece hard plastic walker body, blonde wig pulled atop head, grey sleep eyes, molded lashes. Tagged plaid dress with organdy bodice insert and sleeves, slip with ribbon and matching pantalets, red knit hose, blue straw hat, black side-snap shoes. Circa 1961. #486 Faith from the Americana Series.

237. Madame Alexander Little Women
8″. Set of five dolls, all have seven-piece hard plastic bent-knee walker bodies marked Alex on back. All outfits are tagged and most have wrist booklets. Circa 1965. #781 Little Women set, #381 Marme (1960-63).

238. Vogue Ginny Ballerina
8″. Five-piece hard plastic body, auburn curled wig, blue sleep eyes, painted lashes. Tagged multi-colored tutu with flowers, net slip with attached panty, floral headpiece, ballet slippers. Marked Vogue Doll on back. Circa 1953. #45 Ballet from the Gadabout Series.

239. Vogue Ginny
8″. Five-piece hard plastic body, blonde mohair wig with blue bow, blue sleep eyes, painted lashes. Tagged blue dress with plaid trim, attached panty, red shoes. Marked Vogue Doll on back. Circa 1950. Has an unusual eye color only found in very early models.

240. Vogue Ginny Skier
8″. Five-piece hard plastic walker body, brown mohair wig, blue sleep eyes, painted lashes. Tagged green felt ski outfit of jacket with zipper front, pants with attached red top, matching cap, white vinyl shoes. Marked Vogue Doll on back. Circa 1955. #49 Fun Time Series with wooden skis and poles.

241. Vogue Ginnette with Box

8". Five-piece vinyl baby body, molded hair, blue sleep eyes, molded lashes, mouth with bottle opening. Blue and pink nylon clown suit with pompom front, matching hat, tulle neck ruffle, flannel diaper, white vinyl shoes. Marked Vogue Dolls on back. Circa 1956. With original box marked #6570.

242. Vogue Ginny Walker Clown

8". Five-piece hard plastic walker body, brown braided wig, blue sleep eyes, molded lashes. Blue and pink nylon clown suit with pompom front, matching hat, tulle neck ruffle, panty, white tie shoes. Marked Ginny Vogue Dolls Inc Patent No 2687594 Made in USA on back. Circa 1956. Outfit #6041, Tiny Miss Series.

243. Vogue Ginny with Box

8". Seven-piece hard plastic bent-knee walker body, brown curled wig, blue sleep eyes, molded lashes. White panty, socks and pink vinyl shoes. Marked as above on back. Circa 1957. Original box #1001 with booklet and circular wrist tag.

244. Vogue Ginny with Box

8". Five-piece hard plastic walker body, brown curled wig, blue sleep eyes, molded lashes. Blue panty, socks and blue vinyl shoes. Marked as above on back. Circa 1956. Original box #6102 with booklet.

245. Vogue Ginny with Box

7 1/2". Seven-piece hard plastic bent-knee body, brown rooted wig, grey sleep eyes, molded lashes. Nylon panty, socks and white vinyl shoes. Marked as above on back. Circa 1963. With original box #1821 booklet and Ginny hang tag.

246. Vogue Ginny with Box

8". Five-piece hard vinyl body, rooted brown wig, green sleep eyes, molded lashes. Pink cotton dress with nylon overlay, panty, socks, white vinyl shoes. Marked Ginny on head and Ginny Vogue Dolls Inc on back. Circa 1962. #181 with original box.

247. Vogue Ginny with Box

7 1/2". Seven-piece hard plastic bent-knee body, blonde rooted wig, blue sleep eyes, molded lashes. Tagged nightgown with angel print, panty, socks, white vinyl shoes. Marked Ginny with Vogue Patent number. Circa 1964. With original box, color booklet featuring "Negro Dolls" and hang tag.

248. American Character Whimsie with Box
20″. One-piece sectioned, stuffed vinyl body, rooted pink hair with bendable braids, painted intaglio brown eyes, broad smiling expression. Pink gingham dress with ric-rac trim and flower appliques, matching panty, sandals, floral bouquet. Circa 1960. #1008 Dixie the Pixie with original box and tag.

249. American Character Whimsie with Box
20″. One-piece sectioned, stuffed vinyl body, green rooted hair, molded closed eyes, smiling expression. White satin and dotted net "gown", net veil with flowers, panty, sandals, wrist corsage. Circa 1960. #1012 Bessie the Bashful Bride with original box and hang tag.

250. Tinker Bell
12″. Five-piece hard vinyl body with purple glitter wings inserted into the back, rooted yellow wig, blue open eyes, inserted lashes. Green felt suit with glitter accents, yellow panty, painted green shoes with red plastic pompom. Marked Walt Disney Productions Made in Hong Kong on back and bottom of foot. Circa 1960's. Unusual model with surprised expression.

251. Vogue Ginny Brownie
8". Five-piece hard plastic walker body, brown braided wig, blue sleep eyes, molded lashes. Tagged Brownie uniform with felt cap, panty and vinyl shoes. Marked Ginny Vogue Dolls Inc Patent No 2687594 Made in USA on back. Circa 1956. #6032 Gym Kids Series.

252. Vogue Ginny Scout
Same description as above but with out-fit variation of removable belt and no front plackets. Circa 1957. #7032 Brownie uniform.

253. Vogue Ginny Cowgirl
8". Five-piece hard plastic walker body, reddish braided wig, blue sleep eyes, molded lashes. Tagged outfit of aqua cotton top with attached white felt skirt and panty, vest, gold belt, cuffs and "fringe" trim, metal gun, hat with feather, boots. Marked as previous dolls. Circa 1956. #6056 from the Play Time Series.

254. Vogue Alaskan Ginny
8". Seven-piece hard plastic walker 'body, brown wig, blue sleep eyes, molded lashes. Brown plush jacket with attached mittens, matching hood, knit top attached to matching pants, white felt boots. Marked as above. Circa 1959. #1258 Alaskan outfit from the Far Away Lands Series.

255. Vogue Indian Ginny
8". Five-piece brown vinyl body, black braided wig, brown sleep eyes, molded lashes. White leather outfit with fringe and beadwork, beaded headband and necklace, booties, brown baby in papoose. Marked Ginny on head. Circa 1969. #501 American Ginny from the Far Away Lands Series with original wrist tag and wooden sticks.

All Madame Alexander 10″ Portrettes have a seven-piece hard plastic body, grey sleep eyes with molded lashes, blue eyeshadow, painted fingernails and tagged outfits. They are all marked Mme Alexander on their backs.

256. Scarlett
Brunette wig, green eyes, green taffeta gown with matching hat, net slip, pantaloon, cameo necklace, black heels. Circa 1971, #1181 with original box and wrist tag.

257. Queen
Blonde wig, cream brocade gown with red jeweled sash, net slip, panty, pearl necklace, jeweled tiara, gold heels. Circa 1972, #1186.

258. Southern Belle
Brunette wig, layered organdy gown with lace tiers, full net slip, pantaloons, gold heart necklace, white picture hat with tulle and flowers, white heels. Circa 1971, #1185 in original box with wrist tag.

Madame Alexander Storybook Dolls

259. Alice
14″. Five-piece hard plastic body with Maggie face, blonde wig, blue ribbon headband, grey sleep eyes, brush lashes. Tagged blue cotton dress with white trim, white pinafore, attached slip and panty, knit hose, black side-snap shoes. Circa 1970's. #1552 with original box and wrist booklet. Unusual doll with older body style.

260. Sleeping Beauty
9″. Five-piece hard plastic body, blonde curled wig, with flat feet, grey sleep eyes, molded lashes. Tagged aqua gown with gold net overlay and cape, gold jeweled tiara, slip, panty, blue vinyl slippers with gold star. Marked Mme Alexander on back. Circa 1959. Disneyland special made for one year only.

261. Bo Peep
8″. Seven-piece hard plastic body, blonde curled wig, grey sleep eyes, molded lashes. Tagged dress with pink and green nylon, black velvet "vest", organdy bodice and sleeves, pink bonnet, slip and pantaloons, pipe cleaner staff, black slippers. Marked Alex on back. Circa 1968. #783 with original box and wrist tag.

262. Snow White
8″. Five-piece hard plastic body, brunette wig with ribbon, brown sleep eyes, molded lashes. Tagged taffeta and velvet dress with cape, net slip, panty, hose and gold slippers. Marked Alex on back. Circa 1972-77. With original box and wrist tag.

263. Nancy Ann Playtime Doll Muffie
8″. Five-piece hard plastic walker body, auburn wig, blue sleep eyes, painted/molded lashes. Cotton dress with print skirt, attached slip, nylon panty, purse, blue front-snap shoes. Circa 1953. #505 Muffie's Gay Cotton Prints Series with original box (price tag $1.98).

264. Nancy Ann Playtime Doll-Margie
8″. Five-piece hard plastic body, blonde curled wig, blue sleep eyes, painted lashes. Pink cotton day dress with floral trim, pink felt picture bonnet, panty, white snap shoes. Circa 1953. #601 Margie with original box, booklets and wrist tag.

265. Elite Vicki with Box
8″. Five-piece hard plastic walker body, auburn wig, blue sleep eyes, molded lashes. Nylon uniform, felt hat, panty, vinyl shoes. Circa 1955. Nurse uniform with generic box #V-200.

266. Norma Playtown Dolls
8″. Five-piece hard plastic body, blonde sheepskin wig, blue sleep eyes, molded lashes. Cotton print top, ribbon scarf, felt vest and chap-style pants, red vinyl holster belt, metal gun, felt hat, red boots. Circa 1950's. #2011 Cowboy in original colorful box with brochures. Another example of a Ginny-type doll with similar features.

267. Penny Brite Outfits
A Pair of Penny Brite outfits in original packages includes #1554 Chit Chat and #1562 Sun and Fun. This clothing is often mistaken for Betsy McCall's as it is also unmarked and identical in size.

268. Plastic Molded Arts "Album of Americana"

6". One-piece molded hard plastic body and legs with movable arms, mohair wigs, sleep eyes. Clothes are simply constructed pieces of felt and nylon with painted shoes. Unmarked. Circa 1949-1955. Set of four Historical Series 1 dolls in original "storybook" boxes with the history of each doll on the inside. Includes Clara Barton, Mary Todd Lincoln, Molly Pitcher and Barbara Fritchie.

269. Topper Suzy Cute

7". Five-piece vinyl baby body, rooted blonde wig, grey sleep eyes, molded lashes, mouth with bottle opening. Blue cotton playsuit with lace and applique, toy cat and rattle. Marked Deluxe Reading c 1964 72 GX on head, Pat Pend 1 on body. Circa 1964. Tiny drinking, wetting baby with bendable arms and legs in original playpen with booklet in original plastic container.

270. Suzy Cute Accessories

Pair of plastic accessories for the above includes Suzy Cute's Stroller #1279 and Swing Set #1295 in original boxes.

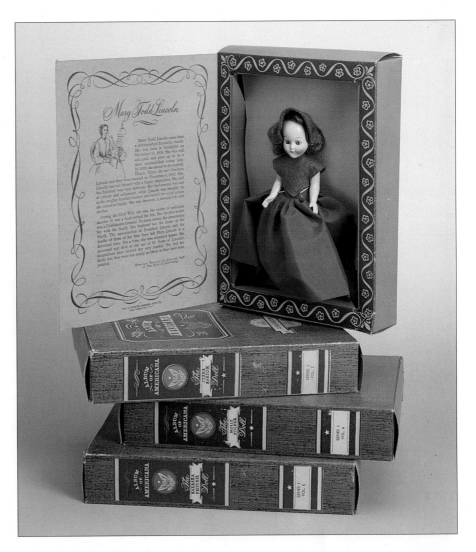

271. Vogue Jill
10". Five-piece hard plastic and vinyl body, rooted curly blonde wig, grey sleep eyes, molded lashes. Tagged pink dotted short nightie with ribbon, open-toe heels. Marked Vogue on head. Circa 1962. #60340 in box with tag.

272. Vogue Jill
10". Same as described above but having rooted brunette wig. Wearing red knit tee with attached white pants with felt anchor accent and rope-style belt. Marked Vogue on head. Circa 1962. #60141 in original box with tag.

273. Madame Alexander Scarlett
8". Seven-piece hard plastic bent-knee walker body, brunette wig, grey sleep eyes, molded lashes. Tagged white taffeta gown with lace, ribbon, ric-rac and rosebud accents, cotton and tulle slip, pantaloons, straw hat with rosebuds and ribbon, black slippers. Marked Alex on back. Circa 1965. #785 in original box with wrist booklet.

274. Madame Alexander Bride
8". Same body as described above. Tagged tulle, lace and organdy gown with matching veil, floral bouquet and head-piece, hose, pink garter and cream slippers. Circa 1971. #735 in original box.

Madame Alexander Internationals

All 8" dolls have seven-piece hard plastic bodies, sleep eyes with molded lashes and are marked Alex on back.

275. Denmark
Circa 1970. #769 with original box and wrist booklet.

276. Swedish
Circa 1965. #792 with chicken in basket and wrist booklet.

277. Dutch
Walker body and Maggie face. Circa 1963. #391 with original box and booklet.

278. Spanish
Walker body. Circa 1964. #795 with original box and wrist tag.

279. Tyrolean Boy and Girl
Circa 1964. #799 and #798 with girl's box and wrist tag.

Madame Alexander Internationals
More of the popular 8" dolls from various countries with seven- piece hard plastic bodies, sleep eyes and molded lashes. All have tagged outfits. Listed from left to right.

280. Peruvian Boy
Traditional attire. Circa 1966. #770 with early, original wrist booklet.

281. Thailand
Brown-skined with ceremonial fashion. Circa 1973. #0767 with original box and wrist booklet.

282. Indonesia
Brown-skined in festive ceremonial costume. Circa 1970. #779 with original box and wrist booklet.

283. Morocco
Brown-skined with elaborate regional outfit. Circa 1968. #762 with original box.

284. Vietnam
Brown-skined wearing traditional, regional fashion. Circa 1969, #788.

286. Marx Miss Marlene
7". Five-piece hard plastic adult body, rooted blonde wig, painted features and shoes. Wearing red polka dot dress and panty (Afternoon at Vassar) and knit turtleneck, capri pants and flannel stadium coat (Winter Frolics). Marked Marx Toys (in circle), Made in Japan and US Patent number on lower back. Circa 1960's. Smaller Barbie-type clones with original boxes.

287. Elite Wendy Fashion Doll
11 1/2". Five-piece hard plastic and vinyl adult body, rooted wigs, painted features. Wearing knit outfits, one with white bathing suit underneath. Marked U on back of head. Circa 1960's. A budget priced Barbie-type in original boxes marked #40.

288. Happy Time Dolls
11 1/2". Five-piece hard plastic dolls as described above. Wearing red knit bathing suits. Marked U on back of head. Circa 1960's. The same Barbie-type fashion doll marketed as Happy Time Dolls #3915.

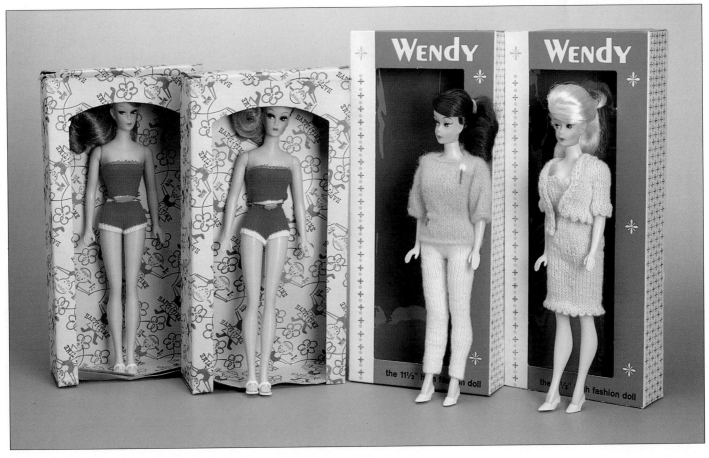

Mattel Barbie and Family Dolls and Accessories
All 11 1/2" Barbie models have five-piece hard vinyl bodies with rooted hair, painted features, molded lashes, painted nails. Stock #850.

289. #3 Blonde Barbie
Original bathing suit, gold hoop earrings, original box, round-based stand and wrapped booklet with black shoes and sunglasses.

290. #5 Blonde Ponytail Barbie
Original bathing suit, pearl dot earrings, original box, stand and wrapped booklet with black shoes and sunglasses.

291. Bubble Cut Barbie
Ash-blonde wig, original bathing suit, pearl dot earrings, original box, stand, wrapped booklet with red shoes and sunglasses.

292. Barbie Adventure Books
Group of four Barbie books including Random House "Barbie Solves A Mystery", "Here's Barbie", "Barbie's New York Summer" and Wonder Books "Barbie Goes To A Party". Circa 1962-64. Barbie and friends adventures in school and away.

293. Advance Barbie Patterns
Pair of patterns for sewing 6 Barbie fashions each with instructions by Advance Pattern Company, circa 1961.

294. Mattel Barbie Magazines
Five Barbie Magazines by Mattel with assorted articles, games, advertisements and advice for Barbie fans. Issues include May/June 1964 (2), Sept/Oct 1964, May/June 1966, July/Aug 1966.

Barbie's best friend Midge has the same body construction, rooted hair and painted features, usually featuring freckles. Stock #860.

295. Blonde Midge
Original two-piece bathing suit, stand, wrapped booklet with shoes and box.

296. Brunette Midge
Original two-piece bathing suit, stand, wrapped booklet with shoes and box.

297. Side-Part Midge with Bendable Legs
Original multi-colored, striped bathing suit, stand, wrapped booklet with shoes and box. Stock #1080.

298. Suzy Goose Barbie Furniture
Group of white plastic boudoir furniture includes large wardrobe closet with many accessories, vanity table with mirror, phone, picture, vanity stool and matching area rugs. Circa 1964.

299. Suzy Goose Barbie Wardrobe in Original Box
White plastic molded and hinged wardrobe for Barbie's clothing. Includes hangers, shoe rack, original purple and pink background, and form for the Barbie Fan Club. Circa 1964. #35/J4421 from the Kiddie Brush and Toy Company, Jonesville Michigan.

Mattel Skipper and Friends
Constructed of 9", five-piece hard plastic child bodies, rooted hair and painted facial features.

300. Brunette Skipper
Original swimsuit, headband, stand, wrapped booklet with shoes, and brush, original wrist tag and box. Stock #950.

301. Blonde Skooter
Original two-piece swimsuit, stand, box and wrapped booklet with shoes. Stock #1040.

302. Ricky
Has molded hair, original swim trunks and jacket, stand, box and wrapped booklet with sandals. Stock #1090.

303. Brunette Skipper with Bendable Legs
Original swimsuit, stand, box, wrapped booklet with shoes and wrist tag. Stock #1030.

304. Suzy Goose Skipper Furniture
White plastic boudoir furniture with gilded accents for Skipper includes hanging closet, vanity and bench, ornate bed with cover and Tutti bed.

305. Francie Travel Case
Six-sided vinyl case for Francie with colored fashion drawings and molded turquoise vinyl top and bottom. Circa 1965.

306. Barbie Record Tote
Black vinyl tote with ponytail pictures on front, pull-out handle and record index inside. Includes three "Barbie Sings!" 45 rpm records. Circa 1961. A hard-to-find accessory with records.

307. Barbie Vinyl Tote
Black vinyl train case-style tote with mirror on inside lid, includes some assorted clothing and accessories. Circa 1961.

308. Barbie Vinyl Tote
Round black vinyl tote with fashion pictures on front, four brass feet on bottom. Circa 1961.

309. Mattel Buffy and Mrs. Beasley
6". One-piece bendable vinyl body, rooted blonde pigtails, painted features. Red polka dot playsuit with panty, red and white sneakers. Holds Mrs. Beasley doll with rooted hair, painted face and glasses. Marked c 1965 Mattel Inc Japan 25 on back. Circa 1967. Stock #3577 from the TV series "Family Affair" with original box.

310. Mattel Todd and Boxed Outfit
6". One-piece bendable vinyl body, rooted red hair, painted features. Blue shirt, red shorts and cap, socks, sneakers. Marks should be the same as above as the same body was used for both. Circa 1973. Stock #8129. Tutti's twin brother in original box with extra boxed outfit #2188 Baseball Outfit for the European market with original 6.95 DM price tag.

311. Vogue Coronation Queen Ginny
8". Five-piece hard plastic body, brunette wig, brown sleep eyes, painted lashes. Cream brocade gown with gold trim, sequins and beading, taffeta liner with lace edging, blue sash, purple velvet long robe with fur lining, heavy silver and gold threaded emblem at the bottom of train, velvet lined gold replica crown with pearl edging, brass scepter, gold slippers. Marked Vogue Doll on back. Circa 1953. Made to coincide with Queen Elizabeth's coronation, Vogue advertised this Ginny as "Queen of All Doll Land-truly Ruler of All the Young in Heart".